KU-394-276

Schools Library and Information Services
S00000724190

My family celebrates Baisakhi

Cath Senker

Photography by Chris Fairclough

W
FRANKLIN WATTS
LONDON • SYDNEY

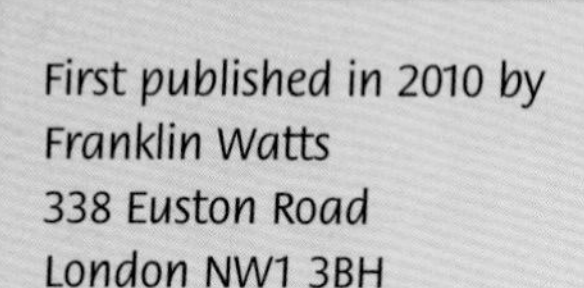

First published in 2010 by
Franklin Watts
338 Euston Road
London NW1 3BH

Franklin Watts Australia
Level 17/207 Kent Street
Sydney NSW 2000

ISBN: 978 0 7496 9064 9

Dewey classification number: 294.6

A CIP catalogue record for this book is available
from the British Library.

Planning and production by Discovery Books Limited
Editor: Laura Durman
Designer: Ian Winton
Photography by Chris Fairclough

The author and photographer would like to thank the following for their help in preparing this book: Harinder, Mandip, Hardeep, Harjot and Kulbir Singh; Brent Sikh Centre, especially Rupa Sokhi and Mr Hunjan.

Please note, the way that people celebrate festivals varies and this book represents the experience of one family. It should not be assumed that everyone celebrates in the same way.

Printed in China

Franklin Watts is a division of Hachette Children's Books, an Hachette UK company.
www.hachette.co.uk

Words that appear in **bold** in the text are explained in the glossary.

Contents

Globe panels

People celebrate Baisakhi in lots of different ways around the world. Look out for the globe panels for some examples.

About my family and me

My name is Hardeep and I'm nine years old. I have two brothers – Harjot is 12 and Kulbir is 10. I love drawing and painting, reading and playing the violin.

My family outside our house. I'm standing in front of my mum.

We are Sikhs. We go to the **gurdwara** to worship every week. In spring, it is **Baisakhi**, the Sikh New Year. This book shows you how my family celebrates the festival.

India

Baisakhi is also the north Indian harvest festival. In spring, the wheat is ready for harvesting. Farmers celebrate with songs and folk dancing.

I'm good at football!

The festival of Baisakhi

We celebrate Baisakhi as New Year's Day because the **Khalsa**, the Sikh community, was formed on this day.

I am growing up to be a member of the Sikh community, so I read my prayers three times a day.

In 1699, Sikhs gathered for the festival of Baisakhi. **Guru** Gobind Singh asked for Sikhs to come forward if they were prepared to give their lives. One brave young Sikh went into a tent with the Guru.

Soon, the Guru came out alone, with blood on his sword. Four more men came forward in turn, and the same thing happened. The crowd grew worried.

Then, all five men came out of the tent, wearing **turbans**. They had proved their **faith** in the Guru.

Our picture of Guru Gobind Singh at home.

The Baisakhi procession

The weekend before Baisakhi, there is a **procession** around the gurdwara. It is called Nagar Kirtan. Lots of people come to watch and to take part.

Harjot and I walk beside a special float that carries the **Guru Granth Sahib**.

Canada

In Canada, during the procession Sikhs give food to the people watching. Others set up food and drink stalls along the route, and all the **Punjabi** restaurants offer delicious north Indian dishes, such as channa masala (spicy chickpeas) and chai (Indian tea).

The procession is led by five men in **traditional** clothes. They are called the **Panj Piare** which means the 'Five Beloved Ones'. They stand for the first five Sikhs who were prepared to give their lives for the Guru.

The Panj Piare lead the procession.

I had my face painted after the procession.

The Akhand Path

Two days before Baisakhi, Sikhs in every gurdwara take it in turns to read the Guru Granth Sahib non-stop from the beginning to the end. This is called the **Akhand Path**. It happens on other festivals and special occasions too.

This woman is reading the Guru Granth Sahib in the prayer hall at our gurdwara.

The reading continues day and night. It finishes on the morning of Baisakhi. We arrive early at the gurdwara to hear the end of the Akhand Path.

Mum and I listen to part of the reading of the Akhand Path.

The flag-changing ceremony

On Baisakhi, the whole **community** gathers at the gurdwara in the morning for the flag-changing ceremony.

First, we lower the heavy flagpole slowly and carefully to the ground.

Every gurdwara has an orange flag called the **Nishan Sahib** flying from a tall flagpole. To mark the new year, we replace the flag with a fresh one.

We all help to wash the flagpole with milk and water. Then we dry it.

USA

Many Sikhs live in California, and around 15,000 people go to the Baisakhi festival. The Los Angeles Convention Centre is used for the celebrations because no gurdwara would be big enough!

The new flag

A member of the community brings out a clean flag, called a **chola**. We put our hands together and say a prayer called **Ardas**.

We are saying Ardas. You can see the new orange chola, ready to be put onto the flagpole.

At the ceremony, musicians play hymns on traditional folk instruments.

Musicians play a drum called a **dhol** and the **chimpta**, which has many bells.

Then the new flag is fixed onto the flagpole, and it is raised up again. People wish each other a Happy Baisakhi and say Vadhaiyan – congratulations!

Everyone helps to raise the new flag.

The service in the gurdwara

After the flag-changing ceremony, we return to the prayer hall. A Sikh priest explains some verses from the Guru Granth Sahib. Then musicians sing the verses and play on the **harmonium**. This is called **kirtan**.

Our friends Sandeep and Simran sing the first kirtan. They have beautiful voices!

After the service, we all have a sweet food called **karah parshad**. It is a sign of the Guru's blessings. We share it to show that everyone is equal.

Today we have nuts, dried fruit and sweets for karah parshad.

Baisakhi food

Everyone who comes to the *gurdwara* shares **langar**, which is Indian vegetarian food. The langar is particularly special at Baisakhi. It's a cheerful occasion and there are hundreds of people in the langar hall!

A team of helpers prepare langar for hundreds of visitors. Here they are making **pooris**.

We eat **dhal**, rice, vegetable curries and freshly fried pooris. For dessert there is rice pudding with sweet, sticky **gulab jamun**.

Malaysia

Since 2005, there has been a Baisakhi Open House in Penang, north-west Malaysia. Non-Sikhs can come and enjoy the festival. There are live bands playing, dance performances and tasty Punjabi food on offer.

A Baisakhi recipe: halwa

We often make a sweet called **halwa** for special occasions such as Baisakhi. Ask an adult to help you make it.

You will need

- 570ml water
- 165g sugar
- 5 tablespoons of vegetable oil
- 300g fine semolina
- 2-3 tablespoons sultanas
- 25g almonds

Please leave out the almonds if you can't eat nuts.

1. Heat the vegetable oil in a large frying pan.

2. Add the semolina and stir.

3. Pour the sugar and water into a saucepan and heat until the sugar dissolves.

4. Grate the almonds.

5. When the semolina has turned a dark brown colour, add the sugar and water mixture.

6. Keep stirring until the mixture looks like a single lump of dough.

7. Add the almonds and sultanas. Spoon into a bowl and serve.

Glossary

Akhand Path The non-stop reading of the Guru Granth Sahib from the beginning to the end in 48 hours.

Ardas A set prayer that Sikhs say at the end of every religious service.

Baisakhi The Sikh New Year festival. Also spelt Vaisakhi.

chimpta A Punjabi folk instrument used in Sikh worship. It has small brass bells.

chola The flag cloth.

community A group of people who live in the same area.

dhal A curry made with lentils and spices.

dhol A Punjabi drum, used in Sikh worship.

faith A strong religious belief. If you have faith in a person, you trust them.

gulab jamun A little Indian doughnut, served in sweet syrup.

gurdwara The Sikh place of worship. Gurdwara means 'house of the Guru'. It is sometimes spelt gurudwara.

Guru A Sikh holy teacher. There were 10 human Gurus.

Guru Granth Sahib The Sikh holy book. After the 10 human Gurus, Sikhs started to follow the holy book as their Guru.

halwa (say halva) A popular Indian sweet made with semolina.

harmonium An Indian musical instrument like a small organ. One hand plays the keys while the other squeezes the bellows to force air through pipes to make the sound.

karah parshad A sweet food that is blessed and shared out among worshippers at the end of the service. It is sometimes spelt kara prasad.

Khalsa The Sikh community.

kirtan Singing hymns from the Guru Granth Sahib.

langar The dining hall in the gurdwara, and the food people eat there.

Nishan Sahib The Sikh flag that flies outside the gurdwara.

Panj Piare The first five men who joined the Sikh community.

poori An Indian bread, fried in hot oil so that it puffs up.

procession A group of people who walk together in a line as part of a ceremony.

Punjabi From the Punjab, a state in north-western India where most Sikhs live.

traditional Something that is part of the beliefs or customs of a group of people and has not changed for a very long time.

turban A long piece of cloth that Sikh males wrap around their heads to cover their hair.

Finding out more

Books

A Year of Religious Festivals: My Sikh Year by Cath Senker (Wayland, 2003)
Festival Time: A Year of Sikh Festivals by Flora York (Franklin Watts, 2008)
I Belong to the Sikh Faith by Katie Dicker (Wayland, 2008)
Introducing Religions: Sikhism by Sue Penney (Heinemann Library, 2006)
Little Nippers: My Baisakhi by Monica Hughes (Heinemann Library, 2004)
Sikh Holy Days by Brian Knapp (Atlantic Europe Publishing, 2007)
World of Faiths: Sikhism by Kanwaljit Kaur-Singh (QED Publishing, 2007)

CD-Roms and DVDs:

Our Places of Worship, produced by Wayland.
This CD-Rom explores six major religions found in Britain. Each religion is introduced by a child who follows the faith.
A child's eye view of festivals 2, produced by Child's Eye Media.
This DVD follows children through their celebrations of various festivals, including Baisakhi.

Websites

http://atschool.eduweb.co.uk/carolrb/sikhism/sikhism1.html
This website introduces Sikh history, beliefs, worship and customs.
http://www.baisakhifestival.com
This website contains lots of interesting information about the festival, with links to Baisakhi recipes, songs and pictures.
http://www.peterbrookschool.com/baisakhi.asp
This website contains information about the festival, with a link to recipes.

Note to parents and teachers: Every effort has been made by the Publishers to ensure that these websites are suitable for children, that they are of the highest educational value, and that they contain no inappropriate or offensive material. However, because of the nature of the Internet, it is impossible to guarantee that the contents of these sites will not be altered. We strongly advise that Internet access is supervised by a responsible adult.

Index